POSTCARD FROM THE PAST

'Resurrecting these postcards, relics of forgotten times and forgotten holidays, was the simplest and most brilliant idea. Tom Jackson combines the images with just a few of the words scribbled on the back, and his eye for the choice sentence, the perfect phrase, is miraculous. Thanks to his assiduous, obsessive work as collector and curator, each one of these postcards becomes a poem, a short story, an elegy for lost England, a work of art' JONATHAN COE

WOOLACOMBE

Yesterday I caught 3 of my fingers in the car door.

POSTCARD FROM THE PAST

TOM JACKSON

4th Estate • London

4th Estate
An imprint of HarperCollins*Publishers*
1 London Bridge Street
London SE1 9GF

www.4thEstate.co.uk

First published in Great Britain by 4th Estate in 2017

This paperback edition published in 2019

1

ISBN 978-0-00-835181-6

Printed and bound in China.

INTRODUCTION

Every summer during the late sixties and early seventies my sister and I had two week-long holidays away from our home in Northampton. We spent the first with our paternal grandparents at a boarding house in Brighton where we rented deckchairs, played shove-ha'penny on the pier, ate 99s with extra sprinkles, rode the model steam train to Hove and marvelled at the stuffed puppies, kittens and squirrels dressed up to the nines and arranged in dramatic tableaux under glass in Walter Potter's museum of taxidermy under the pier.

We spent the second week with our parents staying at a hotel in Spain, Portugal or Menorca. We swam in the pool, got sunburnt and were confined to the games room for the following day. We ate prawn cocktails and black forest gateau, got diarrhoea and blamed it on 'foreign plumbing'. Occasionally we took hot, dusty rides around the nearby town in a cart pulled by a sad donkey. We went to a Roman amphitheatre once, though Mum remained behind reading David Niven's *The Moon's a Balloon* under an umbrella by the pool. We returned to Gatwick or Luton airport in a bumpy little plane with my sister throwing up pretty much the whole way, taken aback always by the deep green of the English countryside. We arrived home to an overgrown lawn and an avalanche of post which made it hard to open the front door.

These cards are archaeological relics of that lost world, a world whose colours were somehow both drab and oversaturated at the same time. A radiant, atom-powered future loomed over the horizon but the ghost of rationing lingered. Foreign travel might be enjoyable in small doses but going beyond the Mediterranean was the preserve of genuine adventurers. You might, of course, travel to Australia to visit your emigrant in-laws but it was a once-in-a-lifetime experience which you relived annually when you got out the projector and put on a slideshow of the snaps you took while Down Under.

TV reception depended on the weather and breathable waterproof fabrics had not been invented. People smoked like chimneys and had gnomes in their gardens. Cars broke down all the time but most self-respecting men liked nothing better than getting the bonnet up and having a crack at fixing them. Phones were immobile and if Mr and Mrs Patterson and their children went on holiday to the Algarve they would be incommunicado for a fortnight. If Mr Patterson's sister became dangerously ill during this time a sober announcement might be made at the end of the news on the World Service asking the family to get in touch.

It was a time of stoicism and small pleasures – a decent ham and mustard sandwich, a well-hoovered B & B, a clear day. You were allowed to moan but excessive emotion of any kind was frowned upon outside a football ground. Hats remained popular among people of middle age and only sailors had tattoos.

Until recently I thought of these things as amusing at best and embarrassing at worst. Ice cream wafers and *It's a Knockout* seemed to go hand-in-hand with the most terrible opinions about anyone who wasn't a well-spoken white man in a sports jacket. No blacks, no Irish, no gypsies.

I wonder now if the baby wasn't thrown out with the bathwater. In a culture where we are constantly exhorted to earn more, to buy more, to travel more, where we eat sugar snap peas from New Zealand and decorate the table with roses from Ethiopia, where we take our jumpers off and crank the heating up while the polar ice cap melts, where minor celebrities eat raw camel nipples on television in an effort to become slightly less minor celebrities and animals are dying off at the rate of thirty species a day I'm growing increasingly nostalgic for Sunday closing and the deckchair.

Which is one of the reasons why I turn these pages and see not only the places I went to on holiday as a child but many of the places I've been to on holiday as an adult: Cornwall, Snowdonia, the Scottish Highlands . . . staying in rented cottages, taking stout walks in the drizzle, drying off in front of open fires and making casseroles using both kinds of vegetable available at the Co-op in the village. The holiday not as a brief burst of excitement in an otherwise drab year, but as an escape from the consumer overload of ordinary life.

I could watch the sea pounding in against the rocks for hours on end – it's an endless source of fascination.

This book is not quite visual art and it's not quite social history. It's a collection of very short and very cryptic stories set in that drowned Atlantis of the sixties and seventies.

There's smut, but seldom outright vulgarity. There's poetry. There's sadness but only by implication. There's humour, usually understated, often unintended and occasionally surreal. There is a dogged refusal to be greatly impressed. Disappointment is met with a stiff upper lip and dry humour by everyone apart from the man who grew too many cucumbers. And there's the landscape, of course, which remains constantly beautiful as Cliff Richard is superseded by the Beatles and the Beatles are superseded by Elton John and Elton John is superseded by Adam and the Ants.

Best of all are those cards with the most minimal of messages which open like tiny windows onto the panorama of a human life.

A robin flew in the shop.

Alone with my lemonade.

Nothing changes.

Mark Haddon

All captions are taken from the back of the pictured cards.
If you wrote them, thank you.

LION ROCK BROADHAVEN PEMBROKESHIRE

C 2321

The best part was when mum got stuck in the toilet.

If anything it is too peaceful; one feels that there is something wrong –
perhaps there is.

Went cockling with the friends we stay with. Great fun. Cooked and ate them last night.

See what you are missing, Fred.

Very dirty and slow running.

The Pier, Bournemouth

B.2015

Paul & Graham have been fined for biting cats in the legs.

The proprietor had an organ a bit like Uncle George's.

Lovely fishing village. We sat in our bras.

SNOWDONIA

I've got to have a private chinwag when I get home. Please no word to Martin. Yes you've guessed. I've been a naughty girl. Please hush hush.

9

Hope the hamsters are being good.

I am sleeping with Charlotte.

DUNCANSBY HEAD, JOHN O GROATS   A2418

We are literally on this photo.

Our sticklebacks died last night.

I think of you when the food is served.

Having a shower at the moment.

MOUSEHOLE

Water is freezing. Weather uninteresting. Hope you are the same. On no account reply to my last letter.

I'm sick to death of beautiful countryside.

Mrs Copley is sitting on our table for meals.

SURFING IN CORNWALL

I wish I could surf all night.

Fistral Beach, Newquay

N.0466

Christopher is showing off his suits to full advantage.

We watched 'Give Us A Clue' in the evening but couldn't get the colour right so it had to be in black and white.

Where I put the little X is where Christine took me on a motor boat.

Rita's house burnt down.

Dad says he is glad everything is alright.

Claerwen Dam, Elan Valley

N.0642L

Lovely toilets.

This is the horrid beach.

If you take enough scrumpy the trees straighten up.

Boscastle, Cornwall.

Photo: D. Noble, John Hinde Studios.

Just been eating jacket potatoes at Tintagel. Sorry Tina.

Bring coathangers.

TEIGNMOUTH

Digs not up to standard but managing with a squeeze. NO BINGO.

My sandals broke in Yugoslavia.

Only the birds for company.

FARNDALE   HUTTON-LE-HOLE   C 1944

I hardly think it's worth the effort.

ALL WITH US ON THE BUS ARE STRANGERS.

I've just eaten a pot of 'Pot Noodle'.

On Monday night I ended up on stage at the King's Hall. Dicky Briggs and I were doing the Can Can.

Here is another postcard of a polecat.

Jean couldn't get her trousers on.

No tea cosies at our guest house at all.

Meg lost her sunglasses down a crevasse.

Murder.

Dear Grandma I hope you are feeding the cat right.

N. WALES TAL·Y·LLYN LAKE

C749

Jonathan was singing away – water dripping down his face.

BRIDLINGTON

We are only 12m from the sea on a crumbling cliff and mum is getting worried. It might be her birthday tomorrow.

Every ruddy customer left the door wide open.

Having a super time riding my favourite pony Satan.

The exhaust on Dick's Viva has collapsed.

I can't explain what it's like here. So I won't bother.

W.R.A.C. CENTRE
GUILDFORD

I pass out next Thursday.

REGISTER HOUSE, EDINBURGH

The weather is perfect, the sky like forget-me-nots.

The Round Church, Cambridge

C.0317

I was sorry to hear of Elvis's death as I know you liked him very much. Hope you haven't forgotten to water my plants.

Most people go to the caves. We didn't.

AN OLD CORNER OF NEW ROMNEY

Well it seems I did have a third disaster.

No sign of the telephone engineers.

We are happily watching other people's tents blow away.

Thanks for everything you have done for me, now I must pull a lettuce from the garden.

Our hotel.

HAVING A GOOD TIME AT
FILEY

Don't know where we're going tomorrow, but we'll end up somewhere.

I think the owner of the mystery voice is GLEN CAMPBELL.

All is well with Andy – so far.

Found our things moved into another room so left in rage. EAT
CUCUMBERS.

I expect you're lost now the World Cup's over. I've sent a Ladybird Book of Aeroplanes off to Nick.

Greetings from **WALES**

We made our minds up all of a sudden. Wish we hadn't.

The black cat has arrived again.

EL ARENAL

I've just locked Chris out on the balcony. He's going mad.

Nothing changes.

A very dry day except in our room.

Pussy has eaten a rabbit.

Would you believe it when walked in the dining room there sat the same Grimsby couple who were in Ireland.

SCHNEIDER SQUARE
RAMSDEN SQ.

BARROW-IN-FURNESS

SIA THE PARK
FURNESS ABBEY

We seem to have picked the wrong weather.

Makes a break – sea air instead of coal dust.

The Museum and Art Gallery, Doncaster

6

Sorry this is a grotty card, but it was the only one in the shop.

We are now sitting down.

Dick is waiting.

CWM BYCHAN ROMAN STEPS

C 1307

We had a look round Harlech Castle this afternoon and nearly got blown off.

75

If I was here I'd be having a superb time.

TORQUAY

We have visited Paignton Zoo and we saw Terry Scott.

Fortunately the gear box on the car has broken.

If it doesn't stop raining soon I shall have webbed feet.

BEAUTIFUL ISLE OF WIGHT VILLAGES

The devil always looks after his own crikey it is hot here.

THE LAKE DISTRICT

I do hope you haven't had any washing go missing.

I've got my eyes on a lad in the caravan opposite.

What did that lady tell us to stuff our peppers with?

Sarah has been swimming but says the sea is too old.

It is almost unbearable for me.

We are sitting on Torquay sea-front eating our packed lunch in the pouring rain.

Sorry I have not written before but I am terribly lazy.

WHITHORN · The Priory   5718

Keeping a watchful eye on No 13.

Hope you have some luck at you know what.

Had another episode with strapless costume in bathing pool.

Meadfoot Beach. Cockington. The Harbour. Torre Abbey Sands

TORQUAY

Darren got stung in the eye by a wasp.

Tower of London.

Buckingham Palace.

Post Office Tower.

LONDON

Piccadilly Circus.

Houses of Parliament.

A crab bit my toe.

The birds here are very large.

We've been on this beach since 10 past 2.

Mum and dad bought me a nice new watch which you can see in the summer.

Climbed to the top of the picture.

CALA MESQUIDA

Have had to have 4 injections in rump.

Alone with my lemonade.

HAMBURG JUNGFERNSTIEG UND BINNENALSTER

I saw you waving all the way down the platform.

Seen any mullet at the fishmongers recently?

I got stuck in my deckchair.

Caesars Camp.

The Harbour.

RESTAURANT

CAFE ROYAL

High Street.

FOLKESTONE

Bathing Pool.

ET.4372

Kingsnorth Gardens.

You will never guess what – the dreaded gas men have caught up with us.

Of course I am not getting brown.

I could watch the sea pounding in against the rocks for hours on end –
it's an endless source of fascination.

Jackie got stung by a wasp didn't we know it.

St. Mawes, Cornwall.

A3E

Have ended up in Cornwall instead of Ibiza – it's a long story.

I've been having breakfast at lunchtime.

Bedlam.

I kept myself occupied by doing some silver cleaning.

RIVER YEALM, NEWTON FERRERS

KNF 104

Can't say we are having a good time.

SNOWDONIA IN WINTER

2BCB

I'm wasting time by writing to you.

Huge hordes of wild sheep, cows and rabbits ready to attack at any time.

My dear cousin is battering me.

This fortnight has been putrid especially for Lynn.

The Promenade, Weymouth.

ET 1985

Bob and I hated it.

THE HEAD OF BUTTERMERE

Air is like wine & I can't stop eating.

New Flats, Gosport.

ET.4339

We are sitting in the car having lunch in front of these flats. Mummy is looking at her watch.

Mooragh Park, Ramsey, The Isle of Man.

Malcolm's face is like the rising sun.

A robin flew in the shop.

There is a shortage of sunshine, sugar and cornflakes.

Tiddler hunting.

The weather has been good except for when we got struck by lightning.

THE HOUSES OF PARLIAMENT AND WESTMINSTER BRIDGE, LONDON, BY NIGHT

There are times when I'm not proud to be British.

Mine was only a hernia.

I call our tent Slaughter Corner.

SUNSET AT LAND'S END

Went to Lands End yesterday – Pat, Mary, Graham, me and another bloke. I have lost my pencil case.

I'm sitting here staring at Richard III.

The car looks like Dorothy's.

TORQUAY

Saw Freddie Starr (comedian) today in Paignton.

TEIGNMOUTH FROM THE EAST.

Today we are here in the car having a packed lunch.

Haven't really seen too many horses.

THE HARBOUR, PORTMADOC

Dad went into quick sand up to his knees. Mum had made some cheese.

Canoe Lake, Southsea   S.4301L

Paul's bald spot got sunburnt.

CARISBROOKE CASTLE I.O.W.

The second day Ian smashed a flower pot. Bobby is not having anything to do with us.

Surf bathing

CT2314

Plenty of hippies on the pier, but they behave.

Me and Julie went to Eastbourne to a disco everyone was in jeans apart from me and Julie, so we kept our coats on all night.

CHRISTCHURCH PRIORY

We went to catch crabs. It is hard pulling them up.

CONWAY CASTLE AND BRIDGE

Saw Donald Sinden in a cafe here – he was sitting at the next table.

Tomorrow will probably be the worst day for stiffness.

I dread coming back to work, although I can't wait to get home for other reasons.

Looks like being a dirty evening. Stonehenge tomorrow.

Better get those shoes ready 'oh dear God'.

It was kind of you to let me know how your cold was.

At the B & B there was a Dutch couple there and Dad liked the girl and
he said we are going to Holland next I don't think we are though.

No one can call Gladys a dipper, she's a real soaker.

We went with two kites and came home with one.

Quayside, Brixham.

B9D

The scenery here is unbelievable. There's miles and miles of it.

Holy Loch with Polaris Depot Ship and Submarine

D.0835

The hotel is lovely with two gorgeous boys, which are the waiters
the one that Carol likes is the one that serves us.

Nattering & knitting & doing as you damn well pleasey.

Fountain and Spa Bridge, Scarborough

S.0246

Harry had a fall on the crazy golf & has had his knee dressed at the hospital, also two fingers.

39265 PROMENADE AND BEACH. LOOKING EAST, SEATON.

Jean gets off with all the men.

Greetings from RYDE Isle of Wight

Hughie is only one and a half years of age and already he drinks beer as if it is lemonade.

Sandra & I tried brass rubbing today.

SUFF/52 WALBERSWICK CHURCH.   Promise

Mrs Hoddell has a dog now. She is not worried about the snakes.

The Castle by floodlight, Scarborough

S.0292

The hem of my skirt came unravelled and I fell down a pot hole in the road.

All the unused deck-chairs are chained down.

PICCADILLY CIRCUS, LONDON

I'm having a lovely time here in Croydon.

You can tell Maureen was here.

Life here is full of tomorrows.

We've drowned ourselves in cream.

This is the last you will hear of me.

POSTCARD LOCATIONS

Cover Slapton Sands, Devon
ii Woolacombe, Devon
1 Lion Rock, Broadhaven, Pembrokeshire, Wales
2 Lorna Doone Farm, Malmsmead, Exmoor
3 Falmouth, Cornwall
4 Los Gigantes, Tenerife
5 Dovedale, Derbyshire
6 Bournemouth, Dorset
7 Saint-Jean-du-Gard, Gard, France
8 Loch Morlich, Inverness-shire, Scotland
9 Snowdonia, Wales
10 Cheddar Gorge, Somerset
11 Loulé, Algarve, Portugal
12 Duncansby Head, John o'Groats, Scotland
13 Harrogate, Yorkshire
14 Torremolinos, Malaga, Spain
15 Devon
16 Mousehole, Cornwall
17 An Teallach, near Dundonnell, Ross-shire, Scotland
18 Keswick, Cumbria
19 Cornwall
20 Fistral Beach, Newquay, Cornwall
21 The Eildon Hills, Melrose, Scotland
22 Hastings & St Leonards, East Sussex
23 Widecombe-in-the-Moor, Devon
24 Southsea, Hampshire
25 Claerwen Dam, Elan Valley, Wales
26 Ladram Bay, near Sidmouth, Devon
27 Green Beach, Clevedon, Somerset
28 Boscastle, Cornwall
29 Lake Annecy, Haute-Savoie, France
30 Teignmouth, Devon
31 Freudenstadt, Baden-Württemberg, Germany
32 Watersmeet, Lynmouth, Devon
33 Hutton-le-Hole, Farndale, North Yorkshire
34 Seatoller, Borrowdale, Cumbria
35 The River Lyn, Lynmouth, Devon
36 New Quay, Ceredigion, Wales
37 *mustela putorius*
38 Lindisfarne Castle, Holy Island, Northumberland

39 The Bay, Combe Martin, Devon
40 The Grossglockner High Alpine Road, Austria
41 Weymouth, Dorset
42 Bognor Regis, West Sussex
43 Tal-y-Llyn Lake, Gwynedd, Wales
44 Bridlington, Yorkshire
45 Afon Gwyrfai, Waenfawr, Caernarvonshire, Wales
46 Bickleigh, Devon
47 Wasdale, Cumbria
48 St Mary's, Scilly Isles
49 Guildford, Surrey
50 Edinburgh, Scotland
51 Cambridge
52 Cala Figuera, Mallorca, Spain
53 New Romney, Kent
54 Pentre Ifan Cromlech, Pembrokeshire, Wales
55 The Cuillins, Sligachan, Isle of Skye, Scotland
56 Folkestone, Kent
57 Woolacombe, Devon
58 Filey, Yorkshire
59 Edinburgh, Scotland
60 Nottingham
61 Loch Assynt, near Lochinver, Sutherland, Scotland
62 London
63 Wales
64 Caerphilly, Glamorgan, Wales
65 El Arenal, Mallorca, Spain
66 Gyllyngvase Beach, Falmouth, Cornwall
67 Rothesay, Isle of Bute, Scotland
68 Blackgang Chine, Isle of Wight
69 Torquay, Devon
70 Barrow-in-Furness, Cumbria
71 Blackpool, Lancashire
72 Doncaster, Yorkshire
73 Worthing, West Sussex
74 Morecambe, Lancashire
75 Roman Steps, Cwm Bychan, Snowdonia, Wales
76 Paguera, Mallorca, Spain
77 Torquay, Devon
78 Helford River, near Falmouth, Cornwall

79 Wilton Bridge, Ross-on-Wye, Herefordshire
80 Isle of Wight
81 Lake District
82 Bare, near Morecambe, Lancashire
83 Claverton Manor, Bath, Somerset
84 Dartmoor, Devon
85 Benalmadena, Andalusia, Spain
86 Babbacombe & Torquay, Devon
87 Coq-sur-Mer, Flanders, Belgium
88 The Priory, Whithorn, Dumfries & Galloway, Scotland
89 Podgora, Croatia
90 Peasholm Glen, Scarborough, North Yorkshire
91 Torquay, Devon
92 London
93 Porth Joke, Crantock, near Newquay, Cornwall
94 Meadfoot Beach, Torquay, Devon
95 Lyme Regis, Dorset
96 Malham Cove, North Yorkshire
97 Cala Mesquida, Mallorca, Spain
98 University of York, North Yorkshire
99 The Jungfernstieg and Binnenalster, Hamburg, Germany
100 Worthing, West Sussex
101 Carpet Gardens, Eastbourne, East Sussex
102 Folkestone, Kent
103 The Island and Towan Beach, Newquay, Cornwall
104 Tintagel, Cornwall
105 Weymouth, Dorset
106 St Mawes, Cornwall
107 Moor Park, Luton, Bedfordshire
108 Central Pier, Blackpool, Lancashire
109 Worthing, West Sussex
110 River Yealm, Newton Ferrers, Devon
111 Snowdonia, Wales
112 The Yorkshire Dales
113 Mumbles Head, Swansea, Wales
114 South Embankment, Dartmouth, Devon
115 The Promenade, Weymouth, Dorset
116 The Head of Buttermere, Cumbria
117 Gosport, Hampshire
118 Mooragh Park, Ramsey, Isle of Man
119 St Michael's Mount, Penzance, Cornwall
120 Hexworthy, Dartmoor, Devon
121 Sanna Bay, Ardnamurchan, Argyll, Scotland

122 Foxes Path, Cadair Idris, Gwynedd, Wales
123 London
124 New Forest, Hampshire
125 Beddgelert, Caernarvonshire, Wales
126 Land's End, Cornwall
127 West Yorkshire
128 Castle and Seafront, Criccieth, Gwynedd, Wales
129 Torquay, Devon
130 Teignmouth, Devon
131 New Forest, Hampshire
132 The Harbour, Portmadoc, Gwynedd, Wales
133 Canoe Lake, Southsea, Hampshire
134 Carisbrooke Castle, Isle of Wight
135 *homo sapiens*
136 Pevensey, East Sussex
137 Christchurch Priory, Christchurch, Dorset
138 Conway Castle and Bridge, Snowdonia, Wales
139 Muker, Swaledale, North Yorkshire
140 Brighton, East Sussex
141 Exmouth, Devon
142 Coney Beach, Porthcawl, Glamorgan, Wales
143 Ightham Mote, Kent
144 Loch Achray and Ben Venue, Stirling, Scotland
145 Saltdean, East Sussex
146 *homo sapiens* and *canis familiaris*
147 Brixham, Devon
148 Holy Loch, Argyll & Bute, Scotland
149 Lake Windermere, Cumbria
150 Scarborough, North Yorkshire
151 Seaton, Devon
152 Ryde, Isle of Wight
153 York
154 Walberswick, Suffolk
155 Scarborough, North Yorkshire
156 Broadstairs, Kent
157 Piccadilly Circus, London
158 Brighton Pavilion, Brighton, Sussex
159 Pamukkale, Turkey
160 Porthcawl, Glamorgan, Wales
161 Bournemouth, Dorset
164 Gillingham, Kent
167 Salcombe, Devon

Parish Church, Gillingham

Dear Auntie, You will be surprised to hear that I am going to prison tomorrow.

POSTCARD PUBLISHERS

In spite of every effort to trace the original publishers, it has not been possible to trace all those who may still hold copyright of some cards. The following publishers have been kind enough to grant permission to reproduce their work: Bamforth and Co., Jarrold Publishing, Judges, John Hinde Archive, NPO, Nigh IW, J. Salmon Ltd. To them, many thanks. Any new copyright information made known to the publishers will be acknowledged in future editions of the book.

Pages:

86, 91: Ashton Reid, Paignton

44, 63, 72, 112, 118, 138: Bamforth & Co. Ltd., Holmfirth © Bamforth and Co.

70, 79, 95, 106, 111, 135, 147: Harvey Barton, Bristol

101, 156: D.V. Bennett Ltd., Lenham, Kent

ii, 3, 5, 21, 22, 26, 30, 35, 36, 39, 41, 50, 56, 57, 58, 59, 60, 62, 64, 66, 67, 69, 74, 77, 81, 82, 84, 100, 103, 107, 108, 113, 119, 120, 122, 123, 131, 140, 141, 142, 144, 153, 167: Colourmaster / Photo Precision Limited, St Ives, Huntingdon

42, 73, 109, 145, 158: D. Constance Limited, Littlehampton, Sussex

Front cover (adapted), 6, 20, 23, 25, 27, 51, 105, 127, 130, 133, 148, 150, 155, 160: E.T.W. Dennis & Sons Ltd., Scarborough & London

2, 8, 9, 10, 13, 17, 38, 45, 47, 55, 61, 83, 121, 124, 125, 128, 146: J. Arthur Dixon, Newport, Isle of Wight & Inverness, Scotland

85: Ediciones ARRIBAS, Zaragoza, Spain

65, 76: Ediciones Bohigas, Palma de Mallorca, Mallorca, Spain

7: Editions Sofer, Saint Maur, France

87: Ern. Thill, Brussels, Belgium

11: Francisco Mas Lda., Portugal

14: Garcia Garrabella y Cia, S. R. C., Spain

48: F.E. Gibson, Scilly Isles

90: D.H. Greaves Ltd., Scarborough

99: Hans Andres Verlag, Hamburg, Germany

143: Hilil, Istanbul, Turkey

15, 16, 19, 28, 129, 137: John Hinde, London © John Hinde Archive

97: Icaria graf., Palma de Mallorca, Mallorca, Spain

46, 78, 110, 114: Jarrold & Sons Ltd., Norwich © Jarrold Publishing

1, 32, 33, 43, 49, 75: Judges Limited, Hastings © Judge Sampson Ltd., Hastings www.judgesampson.co.uk

161: Lansdowne Publishing Co. Ltd., London

157: Miller & Lang, Glasgow

4: P. Marzari s.r.l. Canary Isles

31: Müller Fotokarnten, Freudenstadt/Schwarzwald, Germany

54, 71: N.P.O. Belfast Ltd., Belfast, N.I.

68, 80, 152: W.J. Nigh & Sons, Shanklin, Isle of Wight © Nigh IW

104: Photographic Greeting Card Co. Ltd., London

154: Promise

29: Les Photographies de G. Rossat-Mignod, Annecy, France

37, 53, 126, 132, 134, 136, 143: J. Salmon Ltd., Sevenoaks © J. Salmon Ltd.

34, 116, 149: Sanderson & Dixon, Ambleside

96, 139: Walter Scott, Bradford

92, 102: Charles Skilton & Fry Ltd., London & Edinburgh

52: Talleres A. Zerkowitz, Barcelona, Spain

40: H. Tollinger, Döbriach Millstättersee, Austria

98: University of York, York © University of York

115, 117, 164: Valentine & Sons Ltd., Dundee & London

89: NIP Vjesnik, Zagreb, Yugoslavia

18: H. Webster, Keswick

12: J.B. White, Dundee, Scotland

88: Whiteholme (Publishers) Ltd., Dundee, Scotland

24, 93, 94, 151: UNKNOWN PUBLISHER

THANKS

Thanks first to all the followers at @pastpostcard. I've been thrilled by the extent to which you share my delight in these strange, touching, funny and very nearly lost messages.

Sincere thanks also to Kirsty McLachlan at DGA for her vision and faith in the postcards and where they might take us, and to Tom Killingbeck at 4th Estate for his drive and enthusiasm for bringing the cards to print once again.

Special thanks to Mark Haddon for seeing what I see in the cards and messages, and for agreeing to express that unsettling nostalgia so powerfully in his introduction.

Thanks to my wife Jola for her Sherlockian endeavours in hunting down defunct postcard publishers and contacting surviving publishers. Thanks also to her for her patience in living with boxes and boxes of old postcards and her support in getting *Postcard From The Past* off the ground – on Twitter and now as a book.

Postcard From The Past is in part a ghost story, odd messages from the past breaking through to speak to us years later. I should send out belated thanks to the phantom army of correspondents who took time years ago to put pen to picture postcard. Thanks for the cards.

This little book is dedicated to my father, who taught me to collect.

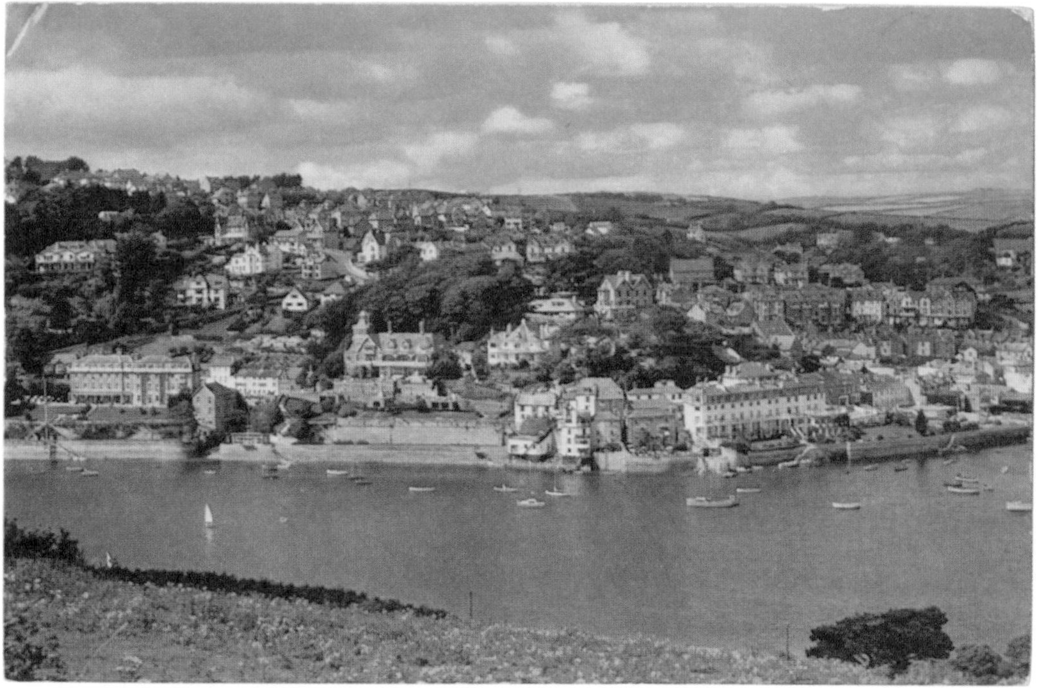

There are no words.